WORKER RIGHTS

EXCERPTED

FROM THE

2011 ANNUAL REPORT

OF THE

CONGRESSIONAL-EXECUTIVE COMMISSION ON CHINA

ONE HUNDRED TWELFTH CONGRESS

FIRST SESSION

OCTOBER 10, 2011

Printed for the use of the Congressional-Executive Commission on China

Available via the World Wide Web: http://www.cecc.gov

U.S. GOVERNMENT PRINTING OFFICE

73–765 PDF   WASHINGTON : 2012

For sale by the Superintendent of Documents, U.S. Government Printing Office
Internet: bookstore.gpo.gov   Phone: toll free (866) 512–1800; DC area (202) 512–1800
Fax: (202) 512–2104   Mail: Stop IDCC, Washington, DC 20402–0001

(II)

WORKER RIGHTS

Findings

• Workers in China still are not guaranteed, either by law or in practice, full worker rights in accordance with international standards, including the right to organize into independent unions. The All-China Federation of Trade Unions (ACFTU), the official union under the direction of the Communist Party, is the only legal trade union organization in China. All lower level unions must be affiliated with the ACFTU.

• The Commission continues to note the lack of genuine labor representation in China. ACFTU officials continue to state that it is their goal to develop stronger representation for workers. In January 2011, for example, the ACFTU announced its plan to establish a system of electing worker representatives in 80 percent of unionized public enterprises and 70 percent of unionized non-public enterprises in 2011. In March 2011, Zhang Mingqi, the vice chairman of the ACFTU, acknowledged that an increase in worker actions was due to enterprises having "neglected the legal rights and benefits of workers" for many years. Multiple localities in China also announced plans to establish collective wage consultation systems in coming years, including Qingdao, Changde, Rizhao, Qinhuangdao, and Shenzhen.

• At the same time, advocates for worker rights in China continue to be subjected to harassment and abuse. In particular, officials appear to target advocates who have the ability to organize and mobilize large groups of workers. For example, in October 2010, a Xi'an court sentenced labor lawyer and advocate Zhao Dongmin to three years in prison for organizing workers at state-owned enterprises. Authorities charged him with "mobilizing the masses to disrupt social order." Authorities continue to detain Yang Huanqing for organizing teachers in fall 2010 to petition against social insurance policies they alleged to be unfair.

• As the Commission found in 2010, Chinese authorities continue to face the challenge of accommodating a younger, more educated, and rights-conscious workforce. In February 2011, the ACFTU released a set of policy recommendations intended to better address the demands of these young workers. Younger workers, born in the 1980s and 1990s, continue to be at the forefront of worker actions in China this year, including large-scale street protests in southern China in June 2011. These young workers also make up about 100 million of China's 160 million migrant workers, and compared to their parents, have higher expectations regarding wages and labor rights. China's Minister of Agriculture Han Changfu has pointed out that many of these young workers have never laid down roots, are better educated, are the only child in the family, and are more likely to "demand, like their urban peers, equal employment, equal access to social services, and even the obtainment of equal political rights."

• With Chinese officials charged with preserving "social stability," the extent to which they will allow workers to bargain for higher wages and genuine representation remains unclear. In part to address official concern over the unequal distribution of wealth across China and its potential effects on "social unrest," the government reportedly is considering a national regulation on wages. Chinese media in the past year reported that the draft regulation includes provisions creating a "normal increase mechanism" for wages, defining a set of standards to calculate overtime pay, and requiring the management of certain "monopolized industries" (*longduan qiye*) to disclose to the government and the public the salary levels of their senior employees.

• The Commission continued to monitor the progress of Guangdong province's draft Regulations on Democratic Management of Enterprises, which reportedly would extend to workers the right to ask for collective wage consultations and allow worker members to sit on the enterprise's board of directors and board of supervisors, represent worker interests in the boards' meetings, and take part in the enterprise's decision-making processes. In September 2010, the Standing Committee of the Guangdong People's Congress reportedly withdrew the draft from further consideration due to heavy opposition from industry. During this reporting year, a major Hong Kong media source reported that Guangdong authorities would approve the draft in January 2011. However, no such action has been observed.

• Chinese workers, especially miners, continued to face persistent occupational safety issues. In November 2010, the ACFTU released figures showing a 32 percent increase in occupational illnesses in 2009, of which the vast majority involved lung disease. Officials took some efforts to close some mines and promote safety, and fatalities have been consistently reduced over the past few years, but uneven enforcement reportedly continued to hinder such efforts. Collusion between mine operators and local officials reportedly remains widespread.

• In January 2011, revisions to the Regulations on Work-Related Injury Insurance became effective. The changes include requiring officials to respond more quickly to worker injury claims, but the effectiveness of the changes is unclear. As the Commission reported last year, the claims process may last for more than a decade. The process is further complicated for migrant workers who may already have left their jobs and moved to another location by the time clinical symptoms surface.

• The extent of child labor in China is unclear in part because the government does not release data on child labor despite frequent requests by the U.S. Government, other countries' governments, and international organizations. While a national legal framework exists to address the issue, systemic problems in enforcement have dulled the effects of these legal measures. Reports of child labor continued to surface this past year. As an example, in March 2011, Shenzhen authorities reportedly found 40 children working at an electronics factory.

• The National People's Congress Standing Committee passed the PRC Social Insurance Law in October 2010, and it became effective on July 1, 2011. The law specifies that workers may transfer their insurance from one region to another and discusses five major types of insurance: Old-age pension, medical, unemployment, work-related injury, and maternity. No implementing guidelines have been released and some critics have said the law is too broad to be implemented effectively. In addition, the extent to which the law will enable a greater number of migrant workers to obtain social insurance remains unclear. At the same time, migrant workers continued to face discrimination in urban areas, and their children still faced difficulties accessing city schools. Employment discrimination more generally continued to be a serious problem, especially for workers without urban household registration status.

Recommendations

Members of the U.S. Congress and Administration officials are encouraged to:

○ Support projects promoting reform of Chinese labor laws and regulations to reflect internationally recognized labor principles. Prioritize projects that not only focus on legislative drafting and regulatory development, but also analyze implementation and measure progress in terms of compliance with internationally recognized labor principles at the shop-floor level.

○ Support multi-year pilot projects that showcase the experience of collective bargaining in action for both Chinese workers and trade union officials; identify local trade union offices found to be more open to collective bargaining; and focus pilot projects in those locales. Where possible, prioritize programs that demonstrate the ability to conduct collective bargaining pilot projects even in factories that do not have an official union presence. Encourage the expansion of exchanges between Chinese labor rights advocates in non-governmental organizations (NGOs), the bar, academia, the official trade union, and U.S. collective bargaining practitioners. Prioritize exchanges that emphasize face-to-face meetings with hands-on practitioners and trainers.

○ Encourage research that identifies factors underlying inconsistency in enforcement of labor laws and regulations. This includes projects that prioritize the large-scale compilation and analysis of Chinese labor dispute litigation and arbitration cases and guidance documents issued by, and to, courts at the provincial level and below, leading ultimately to the publication and dissemination of Chinese language casebooks that may be used as a common reference resource by workers, arbitrators, judges, lawyers, employers, union officials, and law schools in China.

○ Support capacity-building programs to strengthen Chinese labor and legal aid organizations involved in defending the rights of workers. Encourage Chinese officials at local levels to develop, maintain, and deepen relationships with labor organizations inside and outside of China and to invite these groups to increase the number of training programs in mainland China. Support programs that train workers in ways to identify problems at the factory-floor level, equipping them with skills and problem-solving training so they can relate their concerns to employers effectively.

○ Where appropriate, share the United States' ongoing experience and efforts in protecting worker rights—through legal, regulatory, or non-governmental means—with Chinese officials. Expand site visits and other exchanges for Chinese officials to observe and share ideas with U.S. labor rights groups, lawyers, the U.S. Department of Labor (USDOL), and other regulatory agencies at all levels of U.S. Government that work on labor issues.

○ Support USDOL's exchange with China's Ministry of Human Resources and Social Security (MOHRSS) regarding setting and enforcing minimum wage standards; strengthening social insurance; improving employment statistics; and promoting social dialogue and exchanges with China's State Administration of Work Safety (SAWS) regarding improving workplace safety and health. Support the annual labor dialogue with China that USDOL started in 2010 and its plan for the establishment of a safety dialogue. Encourage discussion on the value of constructive interactions among labor NGOs, workers, employers, and government agencies. Encourage exchanges that emphasize the importance of government transparency in developing stable labor relations and in ensuring full and fair enforcement of labor laws.

Introduction

Workers in China still are not guaranteed, either by law or in practice, full worker rights in accordance with international standards, including the right to organize into independent unions. Advocates for worker rights in China continued to be subjected to harassment and abuse. The All-China Federation of Trade Unions (ACFTU), the official union under the direction of the Communist Party, is the only legal trade union organization in China. All lower level unions must be affiliated with the ACFTU.

During the 2011 reporting year, Chinese authorities have faced the dual challenges of accommodating a younger, more educated, and rights-conscious workforce and addressing changes in economic development patterns (including inland growth, fewer workers migrating to coastal areas, rising wages, and labor shortages in some locales). Due in part to shifting labor, economic, and demographic conditions, official and unofficial reports have indicated that workers appeared to have gained increased leverage in the relationship between labor and capital. In recent years, Chinese workers have become more assertive in securing their rights, higher wages, more genuine representation, and better protection under China's labor laws. In some cases during this reporting year, workers continued to channel their grievances through, and to seek guidance, advice, and legal aid from, labor lawyers and advocates. At the same time, authorities have harassed, detained, and sent to prison labor advocates who attempted to organize workers for "disrupting social order." Some local officials reportedly beat and kicked striking workers and labor petitioners, and reports of attacks on migrant workers seeking back pay continued to surface.

With Chinese officials charged with preserving "social stability," the extent to which they will allow workers to bargain for higher wages and genuine representation remains unclear. Principles and different aspects of collective bargaining rights have been mentioned in multiple drafts of local and national regulations during this reporting year, including the draft Regulation on Wages—proposed in part to address official concern over the unequal distribution of wealth across China and its potential effects on "social unrest"—as well as trials and measures for collective wage negotiations in different localities. Some critics, however, have questioned the lack of specifics in some of these proposals and, thus, their eventual effectiveness.

Rights Consciousness, Worker Actions, and "Social Stability"

During this reporting year, Chinese officials have continued to assess the characteristics of the new generation of migrant workers as well as their significance on the shifting labor landscape, public safety, and "social stability."[1] Chinese government statistics suggest that these young workers constitute 61.6 percent of all migrant workers.[2] In February 2011, the ACFTU released a study identifying the characteristics unique to current young migrant workers. The document also provided several policy recommendations for "resolving the problems facing the new generation of migrant workers in realizing their rights and interests."[3] The report notes that over half of young migrant workers are unmarried and that 74.1 percent of them had "studied in school" prior to leaving home. By contrast, only 35.4 percent of the "traditional migrants," those born before 1980, had studied in school.[4] These young migrant workers also are mostly concentrated in secondary and tertiary industries and are overwhelmingly employed by private enterprises (84.3 percent) as opposed to state-owned enterprises (12.5 percent).[5] On average, they receive lower wages (167.27 yuan (US$26) lower than "traditional migrants"); are more likely to sign labor contracts that lack specific provisions detailing minimum pay in line with local regulations; have less employment stability; face "relatively more hidden dangers" in terms of workplace safety; and are less likely to join labor unions (44.6 percent of young migrant workers are union members, versus 56 percent of "traditional migrants").[6]

The ACFTU report provides several recommendations on ways in which the government may more effectively accommodate younger workers' unique life experiences and characteristics. Some of the suggestions include strengthening efforts to tackle wage disparities, advance social insurance programs, provide technical training to increase young migrant workers' competitiveness and ability to adjust to changing circumstances, encourage localities to explore methods to reform the household registration system, and organize young migrant workers into unions and facilitate channels for them to address their grievances.[7] These suggestions appear to reflect the Chinese government's initial ideas to grapple with the aforementioned generational changes, a generation of migrant workers who, as one senior Chinese official observed, have never put down roots, are better educated, are only children, and are more likely to demand equal access to employment and social services—and even equal political rights—in the cities.[8]

Official and unofficial reports indicate that, for the most part, the young migrant workers described above have been at the forefront of recent worker actions.[9] Worker actions have been common in China in recent years, and that continues to be the case during the 2011 reporting year. China Strikes, a Web site dedicated to "track[ing] strikes, protests and other collective actions taken by Chinese workers to defend their rights and interests," recorded at least 32 such actions by workers from October 2010 to May 2011.[10]

As with the spate of worker actions that took place in the spring and summer of 2010 that garnered international attention, workers during this reporting year took action to recover back wages, protest the non-payment of wages, call for higher pay, and, for some older workers, demand due compensation in the cases of restructuring at certain enterprises. Social inequality and the lack of rule of law reportedly played a role in driving low-paid migrant workers to participate in a series of riots and protests in southern China in June 2011.[11] In April 2011, workers reportedly blocked the front gate of a liquor factory protesting the compensation terms during restructuring.[12] In the same month, more than 1,000 truck drivers in Shanghai municipality, reacting to rising fuel costs, protested for higher pay. In March 2011, about 80 sanitation workers in Guangzhou city, Guangdong province, took part in work stoppages to protest non-payment of wages, claiming that management owed each worker from 3,000 to 4,000 yuan (US$464 to US$618) for overtime and other allowances.[13] In November 2010, an "entire street" in Foshan city, Guangdong province, was reportedly "filled with workers," perhaps up to 7,000, as management at Foxconn, a Taiwanese-owned company that produces electronics, allegedly forced workers to sign contracts with terms that many workers found unsatisfactory.[14] Starting in October 2010, about 70 workers at a Japanese-owned factory took part in strikes to demand that the company comply with China's labor laws, including the right to sign contracts and to be compensated with overtime payments.[15]

Chinese authorities during this reporting year continued to harass, detain, and imprison labor advocates and lawyers whom officials deemed to be threats to "social stability." For example, authorities ordered Yang Huanqing, a teacher in Jingzhou city, Hubei province, to serve one year of reeducation through labor in March 2011 for "disrupting work unit order" when he supposedly organized 22 and 33 dismissed teachers in October and November 2010, respectively, to petition in Beijing. Yang reportedly led the teachers to petition against social insurance policies they alleged were unfair.[16]

In another case that reflects authorities' concern with labor advocates' and lawyers' ability to organize and mobilize large groups of workers, the Xincheng District People's Court in Xi'an city, Shaanxi province, sentenced labor lawyer and advocate Zhao Dongmin to three years' imprisonment on October 2010 for "gathering a crowd to disrupt social order."[17] Zhao had allegedly organized workers at state-owned enterprises in Xi'an in April 2009 to establish the Shaanxi Union Rights Defense Representative Congress, an organization that, according to China Labor News Translations, a Web site dedicated to analyzing developments in China labor relations, was "critical of the Chinese [state-run] trade union's failure to represent the interests of state sector employees in restructured and/or privatized enterprises."[18] Prior to Zhao's arrest, Shaanxi authorities had warned that Zhao and others had:

> seriously disrupted the normal workings of Party and government organs and have become a huge potential danger to social stability. They have made use of problems in society, including using old and frail enterprise retirees as cannon fodder to pressure the government. They have stirred up extreme delusions and fanned the flames in an extremely outrageous manner. If resolute measures are not adopted, they will grow into a threatening force and are very likely to wreak even greater havoc to social stability.[19]

FREEDOM OF ASSOCIATION AND COLLECTIVE BARGAINING

The Chinese government prevents workers in China from exercising their constitutional right to freedom of association.[20] Trade union activity in China is organized under the All-China Federation of Trade Unions (ACFTU), a quasi-governmental organization under the direction of the Communist Party.[21] Leading trade union officials hold concurrent high-ranking positions in the Party. The ACFTU Constitution and the Trade Union Law of 1992 both highlight the dual nature of the ACFTU to protect the legal rights and interests of workers while supporting the leadership of the Party and the broader goals and interests of the Chinese government.[22] The ACFTU monopolizes many worker rights issues in China, such as shop-floor organizing and formalistic collective contract negotiations, but it does not consistently or uniformly advance the rights of workers.[23]

At the shop-floor level, the ACFTU's unions remain weak and marginalized. While the ACFTU and its affiliated unions at lower administrative levels sometimes may play an important role in legislative and regulatory development, this role is not matched with power at the enterprise level. Generally speaking, firm-level union branches are weak, non-democratic, and subordinate to management.[24] Despite an increase in legislation and administrative regulations that grants the ACFTU more power at the firm level to resolve disputes, the structural weaknesses of the trade union branches make improvements in trade union autonomy and worker advocacy difficult and slow.[25]

COLLECTIVE CONTRACTING

Collective contracts and some process of collective consultation and negotiation have been part of Chinese labor relations since the 1990s, when state enterprise reform deepened and labor conflict began to increase rapidly, especially in the private sector. The ACFTU has championed collective contracts and collective negotiations as important foundations for trade union work at the enterprise level. In recent years, the collective contract system has received more Chinese government and Communist Party support as part of an attempt to institutionalize a tripartite system of labor relations at the local level between the government, the ACFTU, and the employer associations.[26] Moreover, some Chinese officials have stated in public that collective consultation—and, in the process, fostering more genuine representation for workers—could be an effective way to defuse labor disputes and develop "harmonious labor relations."[27]

In January 2011, the ACFTU published a set of "work objectives" for the new year, stating the organization's goal to "set up trade union organizations according to law to unionize the vast majority of workers[.]"[28] More specifically, some of the benchmarks that the ACFTU document provided include the boosting of national unionization rates at "businesses with corporate capacity to 65 [percent]," and an increase in "the number of union memberships to make up more than 80 [percent] by the end of 2011" and "over 90 [percent] by the end of 2013."[29] Even as the ACFTU supplied quantifiable benchmarks, however, it is not clear how these goals will be implemented in practice. It remains to be seen whether such goals will facilitate the approval of local and national regulations with specific implementation and follow-through directives and measures, as well as the necessary reforms to make unions more representative of workers' interests.[30]

During this past year, the Commission continued to follow developments concerning the Guangdong province draft Regulations on Democratic Management of Enterprises (Regulations). As the Commission reported last year,[31] the draft Regulations would extend to workers the right to ask for collective wage consultations[32] and allow worker members to sit on the enterprise's board of directors and board of supervisors,[33] represent worker interests in the boards' meetings,[34] and take part in the enterprise's decision-making processes.[35] In September 2010, reportedly under heavy lobbying by members of the Hong Kong industrial community, many of whom operate factories in southern China and are concerned with rising production costs, the Guangdong People's Congress Standing Committee decided to suspend further deliberation of the draft Regulations.[36] In January 2011, a source in the Hong Kong industrial community who had met with officials in Guangdong province reported to the South China Morning Post that the Guangdong Provincial People's Congress would "very likely" approve the draft Regulations later that month.[37] Other unofficial sources, however, suggest that the approval process of the draft Regulations seemed to have stalled indefinitely.[38]

Other localities in China also announced plans to establish collective wage consultation systems in the coming years. In Qingdao city, Shandong province, for example, the Qingdao City Health Bureau announced in March 2011 goals to establish a system of "equal collective wage consultation" for all contract workers within three years.[39] In a city with more than 40,000 medical workers, the health bureau's plan reportedly will only cover contracted workers, who number around 5,000.[40] At medical organizations where unions do not yet exist, a government document suggests that workers may choose their own representatives.[41] This past year, other cities that reported plans for collective wage consultation initiatives included Changde city, Hunan province;[42] Rizhao city, Shandong province;[43] Qinhuangdao city, Hebei province;[44] and Guanghaiwei city, Zhejiang province.[45] The Shenzhen Municipal Trade Union reportedly plans to sign collective wage contracts at 550 enterprises in the next year.[46]

The extent to which the ACFTU's stated goals, if materialized, and other local experiments with collective consultation will expand the space for greater and more genuine worker representation remains unclear. At present, the collective contract and consultation system remains weak and formalistic in many cases because enterprise-level trade union leaders are not positioned to serve the interests of their workers. Many collective contracts reportedly solely reflect the basic legal standards in the locality and often are the result of concerted government or Party work to encourage the enterprise to enter into formalistic contracts rather than the result of genuine bargaining between management and the enterprise trade union.[47] Finally, none of the aforementioned actions taken by different localities and the ACFTU have changed the fact that freedom of association does not exist in China.

Migrant Workers

Migrants are generally characterized as rural residents who have left their place of residence to seek non-agricultural jobs in Chinese cities, sometimes in the same province and sometimes far from home. Official Chinese government statistics break down the total number of migrants into those who spent less than half the year as migrants, i.e., those who spent less than six months during the year away from their place of legal residence (61 million in 2010), and those who spent more than half the year as migrants (160 million in 2010).[48] The government estimates that over the next three decades, about 300 million people are expected to relocate to urban areas.[49] As a marginalized urban group, migrant workers are often abused, exploited, or placed in unsafe work conditions by employers who take advantage of their insecure social position and lower levels of education.[50] Persistent discrimination reportedly continues to adversely affect the social, civil, and political rights of migrant workers.[51]

In 2011, migrant workers continued to face serious challenges in the workplace, such as wage arrears and non-payment of wages.[52] They also lacked access to reliable social insurance, specifically payments covering occupational injuries and diseases.[53] Many localities have expanded efforts to provide migrants with social insurance coverage. Figures from the Chinese Ministry of Human Resources and Social Security indicated that, by mid-2011, 838 counties in 27 provinces and autonomous regions, as well as the four directly administered municipalities, had launched what the State Council has called the "new-type rural social old-age insurance pilots," covering 24 percent of the population in these areas.[54] A 2009 State Council document also provided details on ways to make social insurance accounts transferable as migrants move around the country.[55] There still appear to be significant problems in terms of participation (for both employers and employees), coverage, and portability between rural and urban areas.[56] Migrant workers generally are able to withdraw funds only from their individual accounts, losing the larger percentage of their pensions that is paid by their employers. With migrant workers facing uncertainty about whether they will return to the same locale from one year to the next to look for new work, and with the portability of pension accounts highly restricted, some have chosen to withdraw their pensions.[57]

Law on Social Insurance

The National People's Congress approved the PRC Law on Social Insurance in October 2010, and it went into effect on July 1, 2011.[58] The law states that the Chinese government will establish[59] a system of basic old-age insurance,[60] medical insurance,[61] work-related injury insurance,[62] unemployment insurance,[63] and maternity insurance.[64] It specifies the respective responsibilities of employees and employers to fund contributions for different insurance programs. Under the law, both the employee and the employer, for example, are required to contribute toward the basic insurance funds for old-age pensions, medical care, and unemployment benefits.[65] For work-related injury and maternity insurance, however, only the employer is responsible for the contributions.[66] The law also requires employers to register employees with social insurance agencies within 30 days of hire,[67] delineates the legal penalties for an employer who fails to contribute the required funds within the specified time limit,[68] and grants social insurance agencies the right to seek help from government administrative units— at the county level or above—to request the transfer of funds equal to the amount of missed payments from the appropriate banking and financial institutions.[69]

One of the law's stated aims is to make social insurance coverage "sustainable,"[70] and the law specifies that workers may transfer their accounts as they move from one region to another. It explicitly states that "rural residents entering cities to work may participate in social insurance."[71] In the cases of old-age and medical insurance, the law seeks to enable their portability by stating that, for an individual who travels from one region to another for work, his or her basic old-age and medical insurance records "will transfer along with the individual," and the calculation of his or her contributions will be "cumulative."[72] Once the individual reaches retirement age, basic old-age insurance benefits will be calculated by taking into account work performed in all localities, but payments will be made in a "unified" way (i.e., no distinction between work done in rural and urban areas).[73] The law, however, states only that "national coordination" of old-age insurance pools and "provincial coordination" of the other four insurance pools will be "gradually implemented," leaving the "specific time frame [and] steps" for the State Council to decide.[74] Moreover, one foreign law firm pointed out that since the law does not provide "national united social insurance contribution rates . . . employers would still need to refer to the local regulations for contribution rates of the social insurance schemes."[75] At this point, the law's effectiveness and ability to standardize and expand China's social safety net remain unclear and implementation regulations have yet to be issued.[76]

Wages

By the end of 2010, 30 provinces had reportedly raised minimum wage levels by an average of 22.8 percent.[77] Some localities continued to establish higher levels of increases thereafter.[78] On March 1, 2011, Guangdong province announced a four-tier minimum wage level chart, categorizing minimum wage levels by region within the province.[79] Authorities assigned Guangzhou city, the provincial capital, a level of 1,300 yuan (US$200) per month. Dongguan city, where many foreign-invested factories are located, fell into the second category, with a new minimum wage level of 1,100 yuan (US$170) per month. In Shenzhen, effective April 1, 2011, the government raised the minimum wage level by 20 percent, to 1,320 yuan (US$204) per month, the highest in China.[80] Other localities, such as Shanghai municipality and Shandong province, also established further increases.[81] Reports indicate that some cities proceeded to raise minimum wages because they struggled to attract workers.[82] Despite rising minimum wage levels, however, reports also indicate that inflationary pressure continued: Inflation stood at 5.4 percent in March 2011[83] and 5.5 percent in May 2011, with food prices rising by 11.7 percent.[84]

The PRC 1994 Labor Law guarantees minimum wages for workers and requires local governments to set wage standards for each region.[85] The PRC Labor Contract Law improves formal monitoring requirements by tasking local labor bureaus to monitor labor practices to ensure rates adhere to minimum wage standards.[86] The law also imposes legal liability on employers who pay rates below minimum wage.[87] In addition, the law guarantees minimum hourly wages for part-time workers.[88]

Illegal labor practices, however, continue to undermine minimum wage guarantees. Wage arrears remain a serious problem, especially for migrant workers.[89] Subcontracting practices within industry reportedly also exacerbate the problem of wage arrearages. When investors and developers default on their payments to construction companies, workers at the end of the chain of labor subcontractors may lack the means to recover wages from the original defaulters. Some subcontractors neglect their own duties to pay laborers and leave workers without any direct avenue to demand their salaries.[90] The Ministry of Human Resources and Social Security, in conjunction with other government agencies—including the Ministry of Public Security and the State-Owned Assets Supervision and Administration Commission—reportedly formed a "united investigative group" and examined wage arrears problems in provincial-level areas such as Tianjin, Hebei, Inner Mongolia, Jilin, Zhejiang, Jiangxi, Liaoning, Guangxi, Qinghai, and Xinjiang.[91]

DRAFT REGULATION ON WAGES

In part to address official concern over the unequal distribution of wealth across China and its potential effects on "social unrest," Chinese media sources indicated that the Chinese government reportedly has assembled a "basic framework" for a national regulation on wages.[92] The Ministry of Human Resources and Social Security (MOHRSS) began formulating the regulation in 2007, and officials reportedly started soliciting comments and suggestions for a completed draft in early 2009.[93] Some media reports indicated that the regulation would be approved sometime in 2010, though one MOHRSS official later said that was never the case.[94] It appears that deliberations surrounding the pending regulation likely will continue throughout 2011.[95]

Based on media reporting, the draft contains 10 sections, including provisions that delineate the "parameters for collective contracts, collective consultations, and minimum wages."[96] In addition, the draft reportedly lays out standards to determine minimum wage level increases, and mandates certain enterprises to "periodically and publicly release average wage levels, increases, and bonuses";[97] requires that overtime compensation, time off given on days with extreme temperatures, as well as various kinds of state subsidies may not be factored into the calculation of wage levels;[98] calls upon provinces to consider local consumer price indexes in setting minimum wage levels;[99] and establishes a "normal increase mechanism" to "create a system" of collective wage consultations and "open a scientifically logical space for wage increases."[100]

Labor experts cited in Chinese media reports also commented that the draft lacks clarity on certain points. For example, it reportedly does not delineate whether or not employers will be required to answer workers' demands for collective wage negotiations, nor does it lay out the consequences for failing to do so.[101] One labor expert also supported the idea to "link wage increases to the growth of enterprises," which apparently was introduced in an earlier version of the draft.[102]

Reportedly, the draft regulation attempts to bridge the wealth gap with additional provisions such as requiring the disclosure to both the government and the public of plans to adjust salary levels and benefits within what one state-run publication called "monopolized industries."[103] These so-called "monopolized industries" (*longduan qiye*) refer to state-owned enterprises in industries such as electricity, telecommunications, insurance, and finance.[104] Another provision reportedly also would require these enterprises to seek approval from three different government departments before issuing bonuses or raises.[105] One media report suggested that these provisions have contributed to the delay in the regulation's approval.[106] One academic cited in the same report stated that the draft's proposed "interference with or even control of wages through administrative methods are not compatible with the trends of market economics."[107]

PRESSURE TO EXAMINE WAGE POLICIES

In 2011, three developments continued to exert pressure on Chinese officials at all levels to examine their policies on wages: Labor shortages in certain areas, growing income inequality, and the central government's acknowledgement of the need to rebalance China's economy. During this reporting year, the Commission monitored reports of labor shortages surfacing in China's manufacturing centers, particularly in the south and coastal areas.[108] As early as 2006, the PRC State Council Development Research Center found that 75 percent of the 2,749 villages surveyed in China "no longer have young laborers to move" outward,[109] and other reports also suggest that more migrant workers are opting to pursue opportunities in their home provinces.[110] Such developments reportedly have contributed to the upward pressure on wage levels and, combined with other factors, have made some factory owners consider moving their operations further inland or to Southeast Asian countries in order to keep production costs competitive.[111] At the same time, it has been pointed out that "improved productivity can pay for more than half of these wage increases, while the other half can be passed in the form of higher customer prices."[112] Moreover, despite moderate increases, wages actually have fallen for 22 straight years in proportion to China's gross domestic product.[113]

The unequal distribution of wealth received much attention in recent years. The National People's Congress and the Chinese People's Political Consultative Conference featured this issue prominently during their March 2010 meetings.[114] In 2011, the Chinese media continued to report on the growing gap between the rich and the poor.[115] The current "income ratio among China's eastern, central, and western regions" is roughly 1.52:1:0.68.[116] Moreover, the distribution has grown more unequal over time, with rural areas lagging far behind the urban regions.[117] According to a November 2010 Chinese report, the ratio of "urban to rural income" was 2.9:1 in 2001, 3.22:1 in 2005, and 3.31:1 in 2008.[118] The difference between the top and bottom 10 percent of China's income earners has increased from a multiple of 7.3 in 1988 to 23 in 2009.[119]

Chinese officials have appeared more willing to openly acknowledge that a higher consumption rate within China is an important part of the government's efforts to rebalance the country's economic development. The PRC Outline of the 12th Five-Year Plan on National Economic and Social Development, for example, noted that

Chinese officials "must be soberly aware of the fact that the problems of lack of balance, lack of coordination, and lack of sustainability in China's development remain prominent" and that the imbalance in the "investment and consumption relationship" poses a challenge to the country's future growth.[120] More pointedly, Premier Wen Jiabao has also described China's current growth model as "unbalanced, unstable, uncoordinated, and unsustainable."[121] Although some experts have said that reforms can be done in the short term via "administrative fiat," such as "mandatory wage hikes," any rebalancing efforts will be difficult, as "state-backed and private corporate sectors are likely to protest reforms that threaten their margins, as will these sectors' support bases associated with their interests, such as the commerce ministry and the Ministry of Industry and Information Technology."[122]

Occupational Safety and Work Conditions

LEGAL FRAMEWORK AND DEVELOPMENTS

The PRC Law on Safe Production, which took effect in 2002, delineates a set of guidelines to prevent workplace accidents and to keep "their occurrence at a lower level, ensuring the safety of people's lives and property and promoting the development of the economy."[123] Specifically, the law charges principal leading members of production and business units to educate workers on safety issues and formulate rules of operation;[124] protects workers' right to have knowledge of, speak up about, and address work safety issues;[125] sets forth trade unions' rights to pursue workers' complaints over safety issues;[126] tasks local governments at the county level or above to inspect and handle violations and potential dangers in a timely manner;[127] and lays out the consequences for non-compliance.[128]

Workers in China, however, continued to face persistent occupational safety issues, especially those working in the mining industry. On November 9, 2010, Zhang Mingqi, the Vice Chairman of the All-China Federation of Trade Unions, spoke to reporters at the National Mining Industry Health and Safety Experience Exchange Conference and stated that China had 18,128 reported cases of occupational-related illnesses in 2009, which represented a 32 percent increase from the previous year.[129] Of the 2009 cases, 14,495—about 80 percent—involved the lung disease pneumoconiosis.[130] The People's Daily has reported that a total of 57,000 Chinese coal miners suffer from pneumoconiosis annually, and more than 6,000 of them die from the disease each year.[131] Reportedly, "pneumoconiosis is now responsible for nearly three times as many deaths each year as mine accidents."[132]

Miners are limited in their ability to promote safer working conditions in part due to legal obstacles to independent organizing. Collusion between mine operators and local government officials reportedly remains widespread.[133] Chinese authorities reportedly closed 1,600 small coal mines with "outdated facilities" during the first 10 months of 2010.[134] The State Administration of Work Safety issued a directive in September 2010 requiring mine managers to spend time in the shafts with workers in an effort to focus their attention on safety issues; the directive also laid out specific fines for managers who refused to do so.[135] The China Daily, however, reported that some managers skirted the new requirements by handpicking "people to be promoted to 'assistants to managers' and to accompany the miners" in their place.[136]

<h2 align="center">WORKING CONDITIONS</h2>

Workplace abuses and poor working conditions remained a persistent problem this reporting year. Allegations of unsafe working environments, for example, continued to surface at factories operated by Foxconn, a Taiwanese-owned company that manufactures electronic products. In July, a worker died after falling from his dormitory at one of Foxconn's factory complexes in southern China.[137] The Commission reported last year that more than 10 employees committed suicide in 2010, reportedly as a result of the harsh working conditions at the company's production plants.[138] Workers often cited low wages, forced overtime, military-style management, and social isolation as some of the major problems that they face.[139] Reports also indicated that some workers are also exposed to chemicals known to be harmful.[140] In May 2011, a blast at Foxconn's factory in Chengdu city killed 3 people and injured 16 others; the families of the factory's workers complained at the time that Foxconn management "turned down" their demand for "a list of dead and injured."[141] Poor conditions and other workplace abuses also surfaced at other factories, including "routine excessive overtime" that averaged 120 hours per month, use of harmful chemicals, poor ventilation, arbitrary calculation of wages, and mistreatment by management.[142] The Commission also observed one recently published report detailing a past case involving Chinese prisoners who, in addition to doing hard labor during the day, were "forced to play online games" at night "to build up credits that prison guards would then trade for real money."[143]

<h2 align="center">WORKERS COMPENSATION</h2>

One major problem facing injured workers or their family members seeking to receive timely compensation is China's "complicated and incredibly time consuming" work-related injury compensation procedure.[144] Some cases reportedly can last for decades.[145] It is difficult to determine the total number of cases in part because many cases never are reported due to the complicated nature of the compensation process.[146] Moreover, Chinese courts and doctors do not routinely recognize some occupational diseases. While traumatic work injuries and deaths have been widely recognized and reported, experts on workers compensation litigation in China report failure to diagnose diseases like silicosis and failure to recognize that the condition may be caused by exposure to chemicals at work.[147] As a result, the extent of work-related diseases like silicosis remains difficult to measure and report on and, therefore, in many cases goes largely unrecognized.[148]

In January 2011, the State Council's revisions to the Regulations on Work-Related Injury Insurance (Work Injury Regulations) became effective.[149] The revisions made 24 changes to the old Regulations, clarifying the definitions of what constituted "occupational injuries";[150] adding law firms and accounting firms, among others, to the list of contributors to the occupational injury insurance fund;[151] and stating that in applications where "the facts are clear" and "rights and obligations are apparent," the social insurance administrative department shall render a decision within 15 days of accepting the applications.[152]

In addition to the aforementioned Work Injury Regulations, the PRC Law on Social Insurance, which went into effect in July 2011, also addressed the topic of work-related injury insurance.[153] It clarifies that the "employing unit," not the worker, is responsible for contributing to the work-related injury insurance fund.[154] The law states that the contribution rates will be determined by the "risk level" of each industry, as well as the number of workplace injury cases that occur in that industry, and leaves the task of setting the specific rate figures to the State Council.[155] Though the law's language maintains that workers are entitled to receive work-related injury insurance benefits if their injuries or illnesses are certified as work related and that certification of such injuries should be "straight-forward [and] convenient," it does not provide a specific time requirement for the certification process.[156] The law does, however, detail the types of expenses that may be paid with money from the insurance fund. These may include, for example, a worker's medical treatment and rehabilitation fees as well as food and travel allowances if the worker obtains treatment outside of the area where the injury took place.[157]

At this point, it is not clear to what extent the revisions to the Work Injury Regulations or the new PRC Law on Social Insurance will streamline the complicated and time-consuming compensation processes for injured workers. Central government directives have, in previous years, encouraged local governments to pressure bereaved families into signing compensation agreements and to condition out-of-court compensation settlements on forfeiture by bereaved families of their rights to seek further compensation through the court system.[158] Moreover, there have been reports of local officials preempting class actions by prohibiting contact among members of bereaved families in order to forestall coordination.[159]

Child Labor

Child labor remained a problem in China during this reporting year.[160] As a member of the International Labour Organization (ILO), China has ratified the two core conventions on the elimination of child labor.[161] The PRC Labor Law and related legislation prohibit the employment of minors under 16 years old.[162] Both national and local legal provisions prohibiting child labor stipulate fines for employing children.[163] Under the PRC Criminal Law, employers and supervisors face prison sentences of up to seven years for forcing children to work under conditions of extreme danger.[164] Systemic problems in enforcement, however, have dulled the effects of these legal measures. The extent of child labor in China is unclear in part because the government does not release data on child labor despite frequent requests by the U.S. Government, other foreign governments, and international organizations. One recent report by a global risks advisory firm, however, suggests that China is rated as "amongst those with the most widespread abuses of child workers" and estimates that there are "between 10 to 20 million underage workers." [165]

Child laborers reportedly work in low-skill service sectors as well as small workshops and businesses, including textile, toy, and shoe manufacturing enterprises.[166] Many underage laborers reportedly are in their teens, typically ranging from 13 to 15 years old, a phenomenon exacerbated by problems in the education system and labor shortages of adult workers.[167] In March 2011, a Hong Kong newspaper reported that authorities in Longgang district, Shenzhen Special Economic Zone, rescued 40 children who were found working at a factory that manufactured electronics.[168] The children were reportedly between the ages of 12 and 14, holders of "fake identity cards" that apparently demonstrated that they were of legal working age, and had worked there for at least three months for about five yuan (US$0.77) an hour.[169] In another case reflective of the child labor problem, Apple acknowledged in February 2011 that, in 2010, it had discovered 91 children under 16 years old working in 10 "Chinese factories owned by its suppliers"; in contrast, in 2009, the company discovered only 11 such cases.[170] In the case of one factory that reportedly hired 42 of the children, Apple learned that the "vocational school involved in hiring the underage workers had falsified student IDs and threatened retaliation against students who revealed their ages during [Apple's] audits."[171]

The Chinese government, which has condemned the use of child labor and pledged to take stronger measures to combat it,[172] permits "work-study" programs and activities that in practical terms perpetuate the practice of child labor and are tantamount to official endorsement of it.[173] National provisions prohibiting child labor provide that "education practice labor" and vocational skills training labor organized by schools and other educational and vocational institutes do not constitute use of child labor when such activities do not adversely affect the safety and health of the students.[174] The PRC Education Law supports schools that establish work-study and other programs, provided that the programs do not negatively affect normal studies.[175] These provisions contravene China's obligations as a Member State to ILO conventions prohibiting child labor.[176] In 2006, the ILO's Committee of Experts on the Applications of Conventions and Recommendations "expresse[d] . . . concern at the situation of children under 18 years performing forced labor not only in the framework of re-educational and reformative measures, but also in regular work programs at school." [177]

Endnotes

[1] See, e.g., All-China Federation of Trade Unions, "The Conditions of New Generation Migrant Workers in Enterprises: A 2010 Study and Policy Recommendations" [2010 nian qiye xinshengdai nongmingong zhuangkuang diaocha ji duice jianyi], 21 February 11; Qian Yanfeng, "Migrant Workers Can Earn Degrees," China Daily, 7 December 10; "Unhappy Rural Workers 'Threaten Social Stability,'" Reuters, reprinted in South China Morning Post, 15 June 11; "Riots Highlight Migrant Rights," Radio Free Asia, 14 June 11; Jeremy Page, "China Stamps Out Southern Unrest," Wall Street Journal, 15 June 11; Katherine Ryder, "China's Labor Market: Valuable Asset or Economic Albatross?" Fortune, reprinted in CNN Money, 17 December 10; Li Li, "Battling for Workers: China's Labor Pool Is Not Running Dry, but Migrant Workers Are Expecting More From Cities," Beijing Review, 8 March 11; "Crimes Committed by Young Migrant Workers Spark Public Concern," Xinhua, 25 February 11.

[2] All-China Federation of Trade Unions, "The Conditions of New Generation Migrant Workers in Enterprises: A 2010 Study and Policy Recommendations" [2010 nian qiye xinshengdai nongmingong zhuangkuang diaocha ji duice jianyi], 21 February 11; Zhang Jieping and Zhu Yixin, "Labor Movement's Demand for the Establishment of Independent Unions Will Change the Country's Trajectory" [Zhongguo gong yun yaoqiu chengli duli gonghui gaibian guoyun guiji], Asia Week, 13 June 10.

[3] All-China Federation of Trade Unions, "The Conditions of New Generation Migrant Workers in Enterprises: A 2010 Study and Policy Recommendations" [2010 nian qiye xinshengdai nongmingong zhuangkuang diaocha ji duice jianyi], 21 February 11.

[4] Ibid.

[5] Ibid.

[6] Ibid.

[7] Ibid.

[8] "Agricultural Minister Han Changfu Discusses 'Post-1990s' Migrant Workers" [Nongyebu buzhang han changfu tan "90 hou" nongmingong], China Review News, 1 February 10. See also "Joint Editorial Calling for Hukou Reform Removed From Internet Hours After Publication, Co-Author Fired," CECC China Human Rights and Rule of Law Update, No. 4, 21 April 10, 1–2.

[9] See, e.g., James Pomfret and Chris Buckley, "Special Report: China Migrant Unrest Exposes Generation Faultline," Reuters, 28 June 11; Zhang Jieping and Zhu Yixin, "Labor Movement's Demand for the Establishment of Independent Unions Will Change the Country's Trajectory" [Zhongguo gong yun yaoqiu chengli duli gonghui gaibian guoyun guiji], Asia Week, 13 June 10.

[10] For more information, see the Web site "China Strikes: Mapping Labor Unrest Across China." According to the site's founder, Manfred Elfstrom, China Strikes is dedicated to tracking "strikes, protests and other collective actions taken by Chinese workers to defend their rights and interests." News reports of worker actions are regularly uploaded onto the site, and they are classified into different categories, such as apparel and textile, bus and truck drivers, machinery and appliance, mines, etc. Data may also be viewed in a map format, showing the number of worker actions that took place in various regions across China. China Strikes, last visited June 2, 2011.

[11] James Pomfret, "Police Stem S. China Riots but Migrant Workers' Anger Runs Deep," Reuters, reprinted in Yahoo!, 14 June 11. See also "Zengcheng Riot: China Forces Quell Migrant Unrest," BBC, 14 June 11; Jeremy Page, "China Stamps Out Southern Unrest," Wall Street Journal, 15 June 11; "Security Reported Tight in Riot-Torn South China City as Unofficial Curfew Imposed," Associated Press, reprinted in Washington Post, 13 June 11.

[12] "Workers Occupied Front Gate of Guizhou Liquor Factory; Restructuring Revealed Protests With Tears of Blood" [Guizhou chunjiu chang damen bei gongren zhanling, gaizhi jiekai xuelei kangyi], Workers Forum, 27 April 11.

[13] China Labour Bulletin, "Migrant Worker Union Negotiates Pay Deal for Tianjin Cleaners," 1 April 11.

[14] James Pomfret, "More Problems for China's Foxconn Over Workers' Pay," Reuters, 19 November 10; China Labour Bulletin, "Foxconn Workers in Foshan Strike Over Low Pay," 19 November 10.

[15] China Labour Net, "Workers of Guangzhou INPEX Metal Product Company Limited Call for Support From Japanese Trade Union," 13 November 10.

[16] "Assembly of Private Teachers in Ten-Some Counties and Municipalities in Hubei Province Calls for Release of Yang Huanqing, Who Was Sent to Reeducation Through Labor" [Hubei shiyu xian shi minshi jihui yaoqiu jiefang bei laogai de yang huanqing], Boxun, 28 March 11.

[17] "Labor Lawyer Imprisoned in Xi'an for Organizing Against Corrupt Privatization of State Enterprises," China Labor News Translations, 10 January 11; "Xi'an Rights Defender Zhao Dongmin Detained; Applied for the Establishment of 'Workers Defense Congress'" [Shenqing chengli "gongwei hui" xi'an weiquan renshi zhao dongmin bei xingju], Radio Free Asia, 27 August 09; "No Trial for Labor Activist," Radio Free Asia, 8 September 10.

[18] "Labor Lawyer Imprisoned in Xi'an for Organizing Against Corrupt Privatization of State Enterprises," China Labor News Translations, 10 January 11; China Study Group, "Zhao Dongmin Sentenced to Three Years," 25 October 10. See also Utopia, "A Discussion With the Compatriots Who Care for and Love Zhao Dongmin" [Yu guanxin he aihu zhao dongmin de tongzhimen shangque], 23 October 10.

[19] Utopia, "Sunshine Is the Best Disinfectant and Antiseptic" [Yangguang shi zuihao de shajun fangfuji], 26 October 10.

[20] PRC Constitution, issued 4 December 82, amended 12 April 88, 29 March 93, 15 March 99, 14 March 04, art. 35.

[21] Bill Taylor and Qi Li, "Is the ACFTU a Union and Does It Matter?" Journal of Industrial Relations, Vol. 49, No. 5 (2007), 701–15.

[22] PRC Trade Union Law, enacted and effective 3 April 92, amended 27 October 01; Constitution of the Chinese Trade Unions, adopted 26 September 03, amended 21 October 08.

[23] See, e.g., Qiu Liben, "The Silent Lambs Are No Longer Silent" [Chenmo de gaoyang buzai chenmo], Asiaweek, 13 June 10; Keith Bradsher, "A Labor Movement Stirs in China," New York Times, 10 June 10; Yu Jianrong, "No Social Stability Without Labor Protection," China Media Project, 15 June 10; Mingwei Liu, "Chinese Employment Relations and Trade Unions in Transition," Ph.D. Dissertation, Cornell University, School of Industrial and Labor Relations, January 2009; China Labour Bulletin, "Protecting Workers' Rights or Serving the Party: The Way Forward for China's Trade Union," March 2009.

[24] Han Dongfang, "China's Main Union Is Yet To Earn Its Job," Guardian, 26 June 11; Anita Chan, "Labor Unrest and Role of Unions," China Daily, 18 June 10; China Labour Bulletin, "Protecting Workers' Rights or Serving the Party: The Way Forward for China's Trade Union," March 2009.

[25] International Trade Union Confederation, "China," in Asia and the Pacific, an Annual Survey of Violations of Trade Union Rights (2009).

[26] Simon Clarke et al., "Collective Consultation and Industrial Relations in China," British Journal of Industrial Relations, Vol. 42, No. 2 (2004), 235, 240.

[27] Yang Lin, "Grasp the Opportunity To Reevaluate the Structure of Labor and Management, Eliminate Contradictions and Hidden Dangers in Labor and Management, and Adjust Policy" [Zhua zhu chongxin shenshi laozi geju, xiaochu laozi maodun yinhuan, tiaozheng laogong zhengce de jihui], Outlook, 16 December 09.

[28] All-China Federation of Trade Unions, "Chinese Trade Unions Make Progress in 2010," 31 January 11.

[29] Ibid.

[30] Ibid.

[31] CECC, 2010 Annual Report, 10 October 10, 76–77.

[32] Guangdong Province People's Congress Standing Committee, "Opinions From the Public Openly Sought for 'Guangdong Province's Regulations on Enterprise Democratic Management (Third Draft for Public Comment)'" [Guangdong sheng qiye minzhu guanli tiaoli cao'an xiugai (san gao zhengqiu yijian gao) xiang shehui gongkai zhengqiu yijian], 23 August 10, art. 36.

[33] Ibid., art. 34.

[34] Ibid., art. 32.

[35] Ibid.

[36] "Guangdong Decides To Delay 'Regulations on Democratic Management of Enterprises'" [Guangdong jue huan shen qiye minzhu guanli tiaoli], Wen Wei Po, 18 September 10.

[37] Denise Tsang, "Collective Wage Bargaining Plan To Start Next Month," South China Morning Post, 15 January 11.

[38] CECC Staff Interview.

[39] Qingdao Public Health Bureau, "The Wages of Contract Nurses in Qingdao Can Be Settled Through Collective Consultation" [Qingdao hetongzhi hushi gongzi ke jiti xieshang], 18 April 11; China Labour Bulletin, "The Wages of Health Contract Workers in Qingdao Can Be Settled Through Collective Consultation" [Qingdao weisheng hetonggong gongzi ke jiti xieshang], 22 March 11.

[40] Ibid.

[41] Qingdao Public Health Bureau, "The Wages of Contract Nurses in Qingdao Can Be Settled Through Collective Consultation" [Qingdao hetongzhi hushi gongzi ke jiti xieshang], 18 April 11.

[42] "Changde City, Hunan Province's 'Spring Contract Action' on Collective Wage Consultation Commences" [Hunan sheng changde gongzi jiti xieshang chunji yaoyue xingdong qidong], Changde Evening News, 29 March 11; China Labour Bulletin, "Cities Across China Roll Out Collective Wage Initiatives," 25 March 11.

[43] Rizhao City People's Government, "'Rizhao City Worker Collective Wage Consultation Trial Methods' Is Released" ["Rizhao shi zhigong gongzi jiti xieshang shixing banfa" chutai], 9 March 11; China Labour Bulletin, "Cities Across China Roll Out Collective Wage Initiatives," 25 March 11.

[44] "Qinhuangdao Year of Collective Wage Consultations Hundred-Day Action Commences" [Qinhuangdao gongzi jiti xieshang tuijin nian huodong qidong], Hebei News Net, reprinted in China Worker Net, 12 April 11; China Labour Bulletin, "Cities Across China Roll Out Collective Wage Initiatives," 25 March 11.

[45] China Labour Bulletin, "Lighter Enterprise in Guanhaiwei Town in Cixi Experiments With Collective Consultation" [Cixi guanhaiwei zhen huo ji hangye shixing gongzi jiti xieshang], 24 March 11.

[46] China Labour Bulletin, "Shenzhen Trade Union Announces Major Push for Collective Wage Negotiations," 24 March 11.

[47] Stanley Lubman, "Are Strikes the Beginning of a New Challenge?" Wall Street Journal, 25 June 10; Simon Clarke et al., "Collective Consultation and Industrial Relations in China," British Journal of Industrial Relations, Vol. 42, No. 2 (2004), 235, 240.

[48] "China's 'Floating Population' Exceeds 221 Million," Xinhua, reprinted in China Daily, 28 February 11.

[49] "Migrant Population To Grow to 350 Million: Report," China Daily, 31 May 11; "China's 'Floating Population' Exceeds 221 Million," Xinhua, reprinted in China Daily, 28 February 11.

[50] Congressional-Executive Commission on China, Topic Paper: China's Household Registration System: Sustained Reform Needed To Protect China's Rural Migrants, 7 October 05. See also China Labour Bulletin, "17 Migrant Workers Die in Fire at Illegally-Built Workshop," 26 April 11; Zhang Yan and Li Jiabao, "17 Perish as Inferno Razes Illegal Plant," China Daily, 26 April 11; Shenzhen Dagongzhe Migrant Worker Centre, "New Ongoing Violations After the Implementation of Labor Contract Law in China," 12 June 09; Jeffrey Becker and Manfred Elfstrom, International Labor Rights Forum, "The Impact of China's Labor Contract Law on Workers," 23 February 10, 7–10, 18.

[51] For additional information, see, e.g., Kam Wing Chan, "The Chinese Hukou System at 50," Eurasian Geography and Economics, Vol. 50, No. 2 (2009), 197–221.

[52] Zhou Pingxiang, "Ten Thugs Brandishing Steel Pipes Beat 100 Migrant Workers Over Wage Dispute; Eight People Were Injured and Hospitalized" [Nongmin gong shangmen taoxin zaojin bairen weiou 8 ren shoushang jin yiyuan], Yunnan Net, 1 February 11.

[53] "Migrants 'Losing Out on Benefits,'" Shanghai Daily, 28 March 11; Wang Wen, "The Woes of Injury at Work," China Daily, 14 March 11.

[54] Liu Conglong, Department of Rural Social Insurances, Ministry of Human Resources and Social Security, "Latest Developments of the Old-Age Insurance System for Urban and Rural Residents in China," 11 May 11; State Council, Guiding Opinion Regarding the Initiation of New-Type Rural Social Old-Age Insurance Pilots [Guowuyuan guanyu kaizhan xinxing nongcun shehui yanglao baoxian shidian de zhidao yijian], issued 1 September 09, art. 1.

[55] State Council Circular Regarding the Interim Method To Transfer and Continue the Old-Age Insurance Relationship of Urban Enterprise Workers [Chengzhen qiye zhigong jiben yanglao baoxian guanxi zhuanyi jiexu zanxing banfa de tongzhi], 28 December 09.

[56] "NPC Standing Committee Passes Social Insurance Law by Wide Margin" [Renda changweihui gaopiao tongguo shehui baoxian fa], Xinhua, 28 October 10.

[57] Ibid.

[58] PRC Social Insurance Law, enacted 28 October 10, effective 1 July 11; Hong Kong Trade Development Council, "China Enacts Social Insurance Law," 3 May 11; "NPC Standing Committee Passes Social Insurance Law by Wide Margin" [Renda changweihui gaopiao tongguo shehui baoxian fa], Xinhua, 28 October 10; "Social Insurance Law Becomes Effective Next July; May Receive Retirement Benefits in Less Than 15 Years" [Shebao fa mingnian 7 yue shixing buman 15 nian ke bu jiao lingqu yanglao jin], Guangzhou Daily, reprinted in Sina, 29 October 10; "Social Insurance Law Clearly States That Retirement Insurance and Benefits Will Be Gradually Coordinated Nationwide" [Shebao fa mingque yanglao xian zhubu shixing quanguo tongchou], Beijing News, 29 October 10.

[59] PRC Social Insurance Law, issued 28 October 10, effective 1 July 11, art. 2.

[60] Ibid., arts. 10–22.

[61] Ibid., arts. 23–32.

[62] Ibid., arts. 33–43.

[63] Ibid., arts. 44–52.

[64] Ibid., arts. 53–56.

[65] Ibid., arts. 10, 23, 44.

[66] Ibid., arts. 33, 53.

[67] Ibid., art. 58.

[68] Ibid., art. 62.

[69] Ibid., art. 63.

[70] Ibid., art. 3.

[71] Ibid., art. 95. For more information, see "China's Top Legislature Adopts Social Insurance Law To Safeguard Social Security Funds," Xinhua, 28 October 10; "NPC Standing Committee Passes Social Insurance Law by Wide Margin" [Renda changweihui gaopiao tongguo shehui baoxian fa], Xinhua, 28 October 10.

[72] PRC Social Insurance Law, issued 28 October 10, effective 1 July 11, art. 19.

[73] Ibid.

[74] PRC Social Insurance Law, issued 28 October 10, effective 1 July 11, art. 64; Laney Zhang, "China: Law on Social Insurance Passed," Library of Congress, 4 November 10; "Social Insurance Law Clearly States That Retirement Insurance and Benefits Will Be Gradually Coordinated at the National Level" [Shebao fa mingque yanglao xian zhubu shixing quanguo tongchou], Beijing News, 29 October 10.

[75] Susan Deng, "Changes Introduced by the New PRC Social Insurance Law," Mayer Brown JSM Legal Update, 1 December 10.

[76] Laney Zhang, "China: Law on Social Insurance Passed," Library of Congress, 4 November 10.

[77] "Another Round of Minimum Wage Adjustment; Shenzhen Is Moved to Highest in the Nation" [Zuidi gongzi biaozhun xin yi lun tiaozheng shenzhen tiao zhi quanguo zuigao], China Business Network, reprinted in Hexun, 4 March 11.

[78] Ibid.

[79] Guangdong Province People's Government, Circular Regarding the Adjustment of Minimum Wage Standards for Guangdong Province's Enterprise Workers [Guanyu tiaozheng wo sheng qiye zhigong zuidi gongzi biaozhun de tongzhi], 18 January 11; "Another Round of Minimum Wage Adjustment; Shenzhen Is Moved to Highest in the Nation" [Zuidi gongzi biaozhun xin yi lun tiaozheng shenzhen diao zhi quanguo zuigao], China Business Network, 4 March 11; Fang Zhenbin, "Pearl River Delta Region Faces Difficulties in Finding and Retaining Workers" [Zhu sanjiao diqu mianlin zhaogong nan he liu gong nan kunrao], Southern Daily, reprinted in CNFOL.com, 23 February 11.

[80] "Another Round of Minimum Wage Adjustment; Shenzhen Is Moved to Highest in the Nation" [Zuidi gongzi biaozhun xin yi lun tiaozheng shenzhen diao zhi quanguo zuigao], China Business Network, 4 March 11.

[81] Ibid.

[82] Denise Tang, "Guangdong Pay Pledge To Drive Out HK Factories," South China Morning Post, 18 January 11; China Labour Bulletin, "Minimum Wage Set To Increase in Cities Across China," 5 February 10.

[83] Zheng Lifei et al., "Zhou Pledges More Tightening as China Raises Reserve Ratios," Bloomberg, 17 April 11; China Labour Bulletin, "Guangdong Raises Minimum Wage as Inflation Hurts Workers," 28 February 11.

[84] National Bureau of Statistics of China, "China's Major Economic Indicators in May," 14 June 11.

[85] PRC Labor Law, enacted 5 July 94, effective 1 January 95, art. 48.

[86] PRC Labor Contract Law, issued 29 June 07, effective 1 January 08, art. 74(5).

[87] Ibid., art. 85.

[88] Ibid., art. 72.

[89] "Over 100 Migrant Workers Kneel in Front of the Zunhua City, Hubei Province, Government Building To Talk Wages" [Bai yu nongmin gong zai hebei zun hua shi zhengfu menkou xia gui tao xin], Sichuan Daily, 13 January 11; Su Dake, "If I Were the Boss I'd Fail To Pay Wages Too" [Ruguo wo shi laoban ye hui qian xin, you qian cai shi ye mei laingxin suan ge sha], Southern Daily, 5 January 11; Zhou Pingxiang, "Ten Thugs Brandishing Steel Pipes Beat 100 Migrant Workers Over Wage Dispute; Eight People Were Injured and Hospitalized" [Nongmin gong shangmen tao xin zao jin bairen wei ou 8 ren shoushang jin yuyuan], Yunnan Net, 1 February 11.

[90] CECC, 2010 Annual Report, 10 October 10, 80.

[91] "Over 100 Migrant Workers Kneel in Front of the Zunhua City, Hubei Province, Government Building To Talk Wages" [Bai yu nongmin gong zai hebei zun hua shi zhengfu menkou xia gui tao xin], Sichuan Daily, 13 January 11.

[92] Suo Han, "'Wage Regulations' Framework Basically Solidified, but Difficult To Roll Out by Year's End" ["Gongzi tiaoli" kuangjia chu ding niannei nan chutai], China Business Network, 19 November 10.

[93] "Draft of Wage Regulation Faces Pressure From Ministry Committees; Accused of Interfering With Internal Management of Monopolized Industries" [Gongzi tiaoli cao'an zaoyu buwei yali bei zhi ganshe longduan qi ye neibu guanli], First Financial, reprinted in People's Daily, 1 September 10.

[94] Ibid.

[95] Ibid.

[96] Suo Han, "'Wage Regulations' Framework Basically Solidified, but Difficult To Roll Out by Year's End" ["Gongzi tiaoli" kuangjia chu ding niannei nan chutai], China Business Network, 19 November 10.

[97] Zhao Peng, "Draft of Wage Regulation To Be Reported to State Council; Intended To Publicize Wages of Monopolized Industries" [Gongzi tiaoli cao'an jiang bao guowuyuan ni gongbu longduan hangye gongzi], Beijing Times, reprinted in Sina, 29 July 10.

[98] Ibid.

[99] Ibid.

[100] "'Enterprise Wage Regulations' Draft Revisions Near End; Industry Insiders Reveal Draft's Brightest Spot" ["Qiye gongzi tiaoli" cao'an xiugai jiejin weisheng yenei renshi toulu gai cao'an zuida liang], Lanzhou Morning Post, reprinted in Sina, 5 August 10.

[101] Ibid.

[102] Ibid.

[103] Lai Fang, "Will Publicizing Monopolized Industries' Salaries Bring More Equal Wage Distribution?" [Gongshi longduan hangye gongzi neng fou dailai gongzi de gongping fenpei?], Southern Weekend, 23 November 10; "Draft of Wage Regulation Faces Pressure From Ministry Committees; Accused of Interfering With Internal Management of Monopolized Industries" [Gongzi tiaoli cao'an zaoyu buwei yali pi zhi ganshe longduan qi ye neibu guanli], First Financial, reprinted in People's Daily, 1 September 10; Chen Chen, China Internet Information Center, "Social Status, Industrial Monopolies Cause Widening Income Gap," 26 May 10; "'Enterprise Wage Regulations' Draft Revisions Near End; Industry Insiders Reveal Draft's Brightest Spot" ["Qiye gongzi tiaoli" cao'an xiugai jiejin weisheng yenei renshi toulu gai cao'an zuida liangdian], Lanzhou Morning Post, reprinted in Sina, 5 August 10.

[104] Chen Chen, China Internet Information Center, "Social Status, Industrial Monopolies Cause Widening Income Gap," 26 May 10.

[105] "'Enterprise Wage Regulations' Draft Revisions Near End; Industry Insiders Reveal Draft's Brightest Spot" ["Qiye gongzi tiaoli" cao'an xiugai jiejin weisheng yenei renshi toulu gai cao'an zuida liangdian], Lanzhou Morning Post, reprinted in Sina, 5 August 10.

[106] Lai Fang, "Will Publicizing Monopolized Industries' Salaries Bring More Equal Wage Distribution?" [Gongshi longduan hangye gongzi neng fou dai lai gongzi de gongping fenpei?] Southern Weekend, 23 November 10.

[107] Ibid.

[108] Willy Lam, Jamestown Foundation, "2010 Census Exposes Fault Lines in China's Demographic Shifts," 6 May 11; Olivia Chung, "China Labor Shortage Spreads," Asia Times, 29 January 11; Jui-te Shih, "Labor Shortages Spread to More Regions, Industries in China," Want China Times, 17 June 11; Edward Wong, "Chinese Export Regions Face Labor Shortages," New York Times, 29 November 10; Jianmin Li, Jamestown Foundation, "China's Looming Labor Supply Challenge?" 8 April 11; Ma Jiantang, "National Labor Shortage Looms on Horizon," Global Times, 3 May 11; Mark MacKinnon and Carolynne Wheeler, "China's Future: Growing Old Before It Grows Rich," Globe and Mail, 28 April 11. For a long-range perspective on wages in China, see Dennis Tao Yang, Vivian Chen, and Ryan Monarch, Institute for the Study of Labor, "Rising Wages: Has China Lost Its Global Labor Advantage?" Discussion Paper No. 5008, June 2010.

[109] "2010 First Quarter Analysis on Economic Conditions and Yearly Outlook" [2010 nian yi jidu jingji xingshi fenshi yu quannian zhanwang], China Economic Net, 28 April 10.

[110] Kathrin Hille, "China's Inner Landscape Changes," Financial Times, 3 March 11.

[111] Federation of Hong Kong Industries, "Survey Report on Labour Issues Faced by HK Manufacturing Companies in the PRD," 28 July 10. See also Dennis Tao Yang, Vivian Chen, and Ryan Monarch, The Institute for the Study of Labor, "Rising Wages: Has China Lost Its Global Labor Advantage?" Discussion Paper No. 5008, June 2010.

[112] Andy Xie, "Sweet Spot for China's Blue-Collar Revolution," Caixin Net, reprinted in Market Watch, 28 June 10.

[113] Hou Lei, "Official: Wage Share Decreases 22 Years in a Row," China Daily, 12 May 10.

[114] Suo Han, "'Wage Regulations' Framework Basically Solidified, Difficult To Roll Out by Year's End" ["Gongzi tiaoli" kuangjia chu ding niannei nan chutai], China Business Network, 19 November 10; "Draft of Wage Regulation Faces Pressure From Ministry Committees; Accused of Interfering With Internal Management of Monopolized Industries" [Gongzi tiaoli cao'an zaoyu buwei yali bei zhi ganshe longduan qiye neibu guanli], First Financial, reprinted in People's Daily, 1 September 10.

[115] Suo Han, "'Wage Regulations' Framework Basically Solidified, but Difficult To Roll Out by Year's End" ["Gongzi tiaoli" kuangjia chu ding niannei nan chutai], China Business Network, 19 November 10.

[116] Ibid.

[117] Ibid.

[118] Ibid.

[119] Ibid.

[120] National People's Congress, PRC Outline of the 12th Five-Year Plan on National Economic and Social Development [Zhonghua renmin gongheguo guomin jingji he shehui fazhan di shier ge wunian guihua gangyao], passed 14 March 11, issued 16 March 11, chap. 1.

[121] Ray Kwong, "What China's 12th Five-Year Plan Means to the Average Zhou," 31 August 11.

[122] Nicholas Consonery et al., Eurasia Group, "China's Great Rebalancing," 18 August 11. See also, Ray Kwong "What China's 12th Five-Year Plan Means to the Average Zhou," 31 August 11.

[123] PRC Safe Production Law, issued 29 June 02, effective 1 November 02, arts. 1, 2.

[124] Ibid., arts. 17, 21.

[125] Ibid., art. 45.

[126] Ibid., art. 52.

[127] Ibid., art. 53.

[128] Ibid., art. 82.

[129] Yuan Junbao, "Great Progress in Preventing Pneumoconiosis in China's Coal Mines; Situation Is Still Grim" [Woguo meikuang chenfei bing fangzhi qude jiao da jinzhan xingshi yiran yanjun], Xinhua, reprinted in PRC People's Central Government, 9 November 10.

[130] Ibid. See also China Labour Bulletin, "Time To Overhaul Coal Mine Safety in China," 19 November 10.

[131] "57,000 Chinese Coal Miners Suffer From Lung Disease Annually," People's Daily, 11 November 10.

[132] China Labour Bulletin, "Time To Overhaul Coal Mine Safety in China," 19 November 10.

[133] China Labour Bulletin, "Injured Coal Miner Struggles for Compensation," 24 February 11.

[134] "Mainland Closes 1,600 Illegal Coal Mines," Associated Press, reprinted in South China Morning Post, 15 October 10.

[135] "Bosses Who Don't Enter China's Mines May Be Fined," Associated Press, reprinted in Washington Post, 7 October 10.

[136] Wang Huazhong, "Mine Leaders To Send Substitutes Underground," China Daily, 21 September 10.

[137] "Another Foxconn Worker 'Falls to Death,'" South China Morning Post, 20 July 11.

[138] CECC, 2010 Annual Report, 10 October 10, 80; Cary Huang, "Foxconn Worker in Chengdu Suicide," South China Morning Post, 27 May 11. See also "Military-Style Management," Global Times, 24 May 11.

[139] Chloe Albanesius, "Foxconn Factories: How Bad Is It?" PC Magazine, 6 May 11; "Military-Style Management," Global Times, 24 May 11.

[140] Chloe Albanesius, "Foxconn Factories: How Bad Is It?" PC Magazine, 6 May 11.

[141] Liu Linlin, "Families Say Foxconn Not Cooperating," Global Times, 23 May 11; Tim Culpan and Joshua Fellman, "Foxconn's Plant in China Has Fire, Killing Two," Bloomberg, 20 May 11.

[142] Gethin Chamberlain, "Disney Factory Faces Probe Into Sweatshop Suicide Claims," Guardian, 27 August 11. See also China Labour Bulletin, "Waking From a Ten-Year Dream," 21 February 11; Chloe Albanesius, "Foxconn Factories: How Bad Is It?" PC Magazine, 6 May 11.

[143] Danny Vincent, "China Used Prisoners in Lucrative Internet Gaming Work," Guardian, 25 May 11.

[144] Kathleen E. McLaughlin, "Silicon Sweatshops: What's a Worker Worth? The Cold Calculus of Supply Chain Economics," Global Post, 17 March 10.

[145] Ibid.

[146] Ibid.

[147] CECC Staff Interview.

[148] Ibid.

[149] State Council Decision Regarding Amendments to "Regulations on Occupational Injury Insurance" [Guowuyuan guanyu xiupai "gongshang baoxian tiaoli" de jueding], 20 December 10, effective 1 January 11.

[150] Ibid., art. 8.

[151] State Council Decision Regarding Amendments to "Regulations on Occupational Injury Insurance [Guowuyuan guanyu xiupai "gongshang baoxian tiaoli" de jueding], 20 December 10, effective 1 January 11; PRC State Council, "PRC State Council Notice 586 'State Council Decision Regarding Amendments to Regulations on Occupational Injury Insurance'" [Zhonghua renmin gongheguo guowuyuan ling di 586 hao "guowuyuan guanyu xiugai 'gongshang baoxian tiaoli' de jueding"]," 20 December 10, art. 1.

[152] State Council Decision Regarding Amendments to "Regulation on Occupational Injury Insurance [Guowuyuan guanyu xiupai "gongshang baoxian tiaoli" de jueding], 20 December 10, effective 1 January 11, art. 9.

[153] PRC Social Insurance Law, issued 28 October 10, effective 1 July 11, arts. 33–43.

[154] Ibid., art. 33.

[155] Ibid., art. 34.

[156] Ibid., art. 36.

[157] Ibid., arts. 38(1)–38(9).

[158] CECC, 2008 Annual Report, 31 October 08, 52; China Labour Bulletin, "Bone and Blood: The Price of Coal in China," 17 March 08.

[159] Ibid.

[160] See, e.g., He Huifeng, "40 Children Rescued From Shenzhen Plant," South China Morning Post, 26 March 11; Malcolm Moore, "Apple's Child Labour Issues Worsen," Telegraph, 15 February 11; William Foreman, "China Factories Break Labor Rules," Associated Press, 20 April 10; National Labor Committee, "China's Youth Meet Microsoft: KYE Factory in China Produces for Microsoft and Other U.S. Companies," 13 April 10.

[161] ILO Convention (No. 138) Concerning Minimum Age for Admission to Employment, 26 June 73, 1015 U.N.T.S. 297; ILO Convention (No. 182) Concerning the Prohibition and Immediate Action for the Elimination of the Worst Forms of Child Labour, 17 June 99, 2133 U.N.T.S. 161.

[162] PRC Labor Law, issued 5 July 94, effective 1 January 95, amended 10 October 01, art. 15. See also PRC Law on the Protection of Minors, issued 4 September 91, effective 1 January 92, art. 28. See generally Provisions on Prohibiting the Use of Child Labor [Jinzhi shiyong tonggong guiding], issued 1 October 02, effective 1 December 02.

[163] Provisions on Prohibiting the Use of Child Labor [Jinzhi shiyong tonggong guiding], issued 1 October 02, effective 1 December 02, art. 6. See also "Legal Announcement—Zhejiang Determines Four Circumstances That Define Use of Child Labor" [Fazhi bobao: zhejiang jieding shiyong tonggong si zhong qingxing], China Woman, 26 July 08.

[164] This provision was added into the fourth amendment to the Criminal Law in 2002. Fourth Amendment to the PRC Criminal Law [Zhonghua renmin gonghe guo xingfa xiuzheng an (si)], issued 28 December 02. See also PRC Criminal Law, issued 1 July 79, amended 14 March 97, effective 1 October 97, amended 25 December 99, 31 August 01, 29 December 01, 28 December 02, 28 February 05, 29 June 06, 28 February 09, art. 244.

[165] Maplecroft, "Child Labour Most Widespread in the Key Emerging Economies; Climate Change Will Push More Children Into Work," 12 January 10.

[166] China Labour Bulletin, "Small Hands: A Survey Report on Child Labor in China," September 2007, 7, 8; He Huifeng, "40 Children Rescued From Shenzhen Plant," South China Morning Post, 26 March 11.

[167] "Disney Factory Faces Probe Into Sweatshop Suicide Claims," Guardian, 27 August 11; China Labour Bulletin, "Small Hands: A Survey Report on Child Labor in China," September 2007, 15, 22, 25–32.

[168] He Huifeng, "40 Children Rescued From Shenzhen Plant," South China Morning Post, 26 March 11.

[169] Ibid.

[170] Malcolm Moore, "Apple's Child Labour Issues Worsen," Telegraph, 15 February 11.

[171] Apple, "Apple Supplier Responsibility 2011 Progress Report," 15 February 11, 9.

[172] For the government response to forced labor in brick kilns, including child labor, see, e.g., Zhang Pinghui, "Crackdown on Slave Labor Nationwide—State Council Vows To End Enslavement," South China Morning Post, 21 June 07.

[173] Ji Beibei, "Students Say Schools Require Them To Do Internships at Foxconn Factory," Global Times, 12 October 10; Ben Blanchard, "China Urged To End 'Child Labor' in Schools," Reuters, 3 December 07; Human Rights Watch, "China: End Child Labor in State Schools," 3 December 07.

[174] Provisions on Prohibiting the Use of Child Labor [Jinzhi shiyong tonggong guiding], issued 1 October 02, effective 1 December 02, art. 13.

[175] PRC Education Law, issued 18 March 95, effective 1 September 95, amended 27 August 09, art. 58.

[176] ILO Convention 138 permits vocational education for underage minors only where it is an "integral part" of a course of study or training course. ILO Convention 182 obligates Member States to eliminate the "worst forms of child labor," including "forced or compulsory labor." ILO Convention (No. 138) Concerning Minimum Age for Admission to Employment, 26 June 73, 1015 U.N.T.S. 297; ILO Convention (No. 182) Concerning the Prohibition and Immediate Action for the Elimination of the Worst Forms of Child Labour, 17 June 99, 2133 U.N.T.S. 161.

[177] ILO Report of the Committee of Experts on the Application of Conventions and Recommendations, Worst Forms of Child Labour Convention, 1999 (No. 182) China (ratification: 2002) Observation, CEACR 2006/77th Session, International Labour Organization, 2006.

○